NATIVE AMER
OF THE WILD WEST

RED CLOUD

❖Sioux Warrior❖

William R. Sanford

ENSLOW PUBLISHERS, INC.

Bloy St. & Ramsey Ave.   P.O. Box 38
Box 777   Aldershot
Hillside, N.J. 07205   Hants GU12 6BP
U.S.A.   U.K.

4/4/04

Library of Congress Cataloging-in-Publication Data

Sanford, William R. (William Reynolds), 1927–
    Red Cloud, Sioux warrior / William R. Sanford.
       p. cm. — (Native American leaders of the Wild West)
    Includes bibliographical references and index.
    ISBN 0-89490-513-9
    1. Red Cloud, 1822–1909—Juvenile literature. 2. Oglala Indians—Biography—
Juvenile literature. 3. Oglala Indians—Kings and rulers—Juvenile literature.
4. Oglala Indians—History—Juvenile literature. 5. Fetterman Fight, Wyo., 1866—
Juvenile literature. 6. Red Cloud, 1822–1909. I. Title. II. Series: Sanford, William R.
(William Reynolds), 1927– . Native American leaders of the Wild West.
E99.O3R377 1994
973'.04'975'0092—dc20
[B]
                                            93-42256
                                               CIP

Printed in the United States of America   AC

10 9 8 7 6 5 4 3 2 1

Photo Credits: Library of Congress, p. 42; National Archives, pp. 12, 32, 33,
35; William Sanford, p. 27; Smithsonian Institution, pp. 13, 15, 37; South
Dakota State Historical Society, pp. 6, 39, 41; Wyoming State Museum, pp.
8, 9, 18, 22, 23, 30, 31.

Cover Illustration: Paul Daly

CONTENTS

Author's Note 4

1 The Fetterman Fight 5

2 Two Arrows Becomes Red Cloud . . 10

3 Red Cloud Becomes
an Oglala Chief 14

4 A New Trail
Challenges the Sioux 17

5 Red Cloud's War 21

6 The War Drags On 25

7 A Sioux Victory 29

8 Red Cloud Goes to Washington . . . 34

9 The Final Years 38

Notes by Chapter 43

Glossary 45

More Good Reading
About Red Cloud 46

Index 47

AUTHOR'S NOTE

This book tells the true story of the Oglala Sioux chief Red Cloud. Many mistakenly believe that his fame rests on one battle, the Fetterman Fight. His true fame, however, comes from his long-term struggle with the United States. After the discovery of gold in Montana, would-be miners swarmed across Sioux land using the Bozeman Trail. Red Cloud made sure they could never safely cross the trail.

Following his many victories, stories about Red Cloud filled the press. Some were fiction, but others were true. The events described in this book all really happened.

The wars between Native Americans and white settlers lasted over 250 years. In only one case did the United States suffer defeat. The Native American who led his people to victory was Red Cloud.

THE FETTERMAN FIGHT

On December 21, 1866, in his camp outside Fort Phil Kearny, Red Cloud waited. He waited for the medicine man who had ridden into the hills, inwardly searching. He wanted to find out whether the Sioux would kill any soldiers in the coming battle. The medicine man galloped into Red Cloud's camp. He blew shrill notes from an eagle-bone whistle. "I have a hundred dead soldiers in my hands," he cried.[1] Everyone cheered. The Sioux pressed forward to touch the medicine man's hands. Red Cloud was pleased; the medicine man was never wrong.

Red Cloud had a plan. Each day a wagon train left Fort Phil Kearny to get wood. A few of his men would pretend to attack this logging party. Then soldiers from the fort would come to its rescue. The "decoy" warriors would retreat slowly. They wanted the soldiers to follow them. The rest of Red Cloud's men would lie in ambush. Red

The Oglala Sioux chief, Red Cloud, won his war to close the Bozeman Trail. He then led his people onto a reservation and lived for many years in peace.

Cloud hoped the plan would work this time. It had failed a few days earlier when some of his young men had opened fire too soon. This caused the soldiers to stop atop a ridge. Then they turned back to the fort.

Red Cloud didn't know that this day's trip for wood would be the last of the year. The soldiers had worked since mid-July, building the fort. Its eight-foot-high wooden wall was now complete. But the soldiers had almost enough firewood to last the winter. Colonel Henry Carrington was the fort commander. He sent a strong guard for this last trip.

The logging party left for the fort just after 10 A.M. An hour later a lookout signaled. Red Cloud's men had attacked the wagons. Bugles sounded in the fort. An infantry company of forty-eight men quickly assembled. The soldiers carried single-shot muzzle-loading rifles. Their leader was Captain William J. Fetterman. He once had boasted, "Give me eighty men and I would ride through the whole Sioux Nation."[2] The twenty-eight men of a cavalry company joined the infantry. Carrington gave Fetterman his orders. "Support the wood train. Relieve it and report to me. Do not engage or pursue Indians. . . . Under no circumstances pursue over Lodge Trail Ridge."[3]

When Fetterman's force left the fort, the decoys broke off their attack. They retreated north over Lodge Trail Ridge. Fetterman followed to the top of the ridge. Crazy Horse and the other decoys galloped close. They fired at the soldiers, killing one. Then Fetterman ordered the

The Bozeman Trail passed along the top of Lodge Trail Ridge. The Fetterman Fight took place along the road.

soldiers to move north in pursuit. Two thousand Sioux lay in ambush ahead.

One Sioux reported, "We held our horses' mouths so they would not neigh at the strange horses. . . . Everything is still. There is only the clink of iron horseshoes against the stones. . . . The leading soldiers have reached the trail. Now they are between us."[4] Little Horse signalled by shaking his lance over his head. Hundreds of Sioux warriors sprang from behind rocks. A cloud of arrows whistled toward the soldiers. Many were killed before they could fire a shot. The soldiers fell back, making their way to a nearby ridge. Some found shelter behind boulders.

The firing lasted less than an hour. By that time the last soldier was dead. A soldier's dog ran up the trail toward the fort. "Let him tell the other dogs at the fort what has happened here," Red Cloud said.[5]

Lookouts warned that more soldiers were coming from the fort. The warriors melted away. Captain Tenedor Ten Eyck led the relief force. His men loaded the soldiers' bodies into wagons. Then they returned to the fort and prepared for an attack. But that night a blizzard brought -20°F weather. Instead of war, Red Cloud's forces sought the warmth of their campfires.

Red Cloud planned the ambush near Fort Phil Kearny. His warriors destroyed a force led by Captain William Fetterman.

TWO ARROWS BECOMES RED CLOUD

One winter night in 1822 the northern sky flared red with light. To the Sioux, this was a sign that a future chief would soon be born. That night Walks-As-She-Thinks bore a son. Her husband Lone Man placed two arrows on the chest of the newborn babe. This was to make sure that the boy would grow up to be a brave warrior and hunter. From this act the boy gained his childhood name of Two Arrows.

Lone Man was a leader of the Bad Face band of Oglala Sioux. His wife's brother Smoke was their chief. The Sioux (pronounced "soo") tribe got its name from the French. It came from a Chippewa word meaning "enemies."[1] The Sioux people called themselves Lakota, Nakota, or Dakota. In the 1800s, the Sioux occupied parts of what would become five states: North Dakota, South Dakota, Wyoming, Montana, and Nebraska.

Long ago, the Sioux lived in the southern United States. By 1600 they had moved north to southern Minnesota. Later that century they came under attack from the Crees and Chippewas. Those tribes had gained guns from the French. Slowly the Sioux began their move west. The Oglala band was one of the seven major Sioux bands. Oglala means "Village Divided into Many Small Bands."[2]

In the late 1700s, a raiding party led by Standing Bull discovered the Black Hills. The Oglala band that settled there was small—perhaps twenty to forty families. Most of the Oglala traveled by foot. Later the band obtained horses from the Cheyenne. The Oglala began to use horses to hunt buffalo. People spoke of the band's daring and its abundant supply of meat. Soon bold braves from other Sioux bands joined them.

The Oglala homeland was harsh. Its main stream, the Bad River, almost dried up in the summer. To the north stretched the Great Plains. By late May, the grass on the plains turned brown and dry. Prairie fires often filled summer skies with smoke. To the south lay the jumble of carved clay buttes called the Badlands. The explorers Lewis and Clark reached the Sioux homeland in 1804. They reported that the Oglala had only 360 people, including 120 warriors.[3]

Both of Two Arrows' parents died while he was a boy. Relatives wrapped their bodies in buffalo robes. Then, as was their custom, they placed the bodies on high platforms out on the prairie.

Red Cloud's parents died when he was young. The Oglala placed their dead on platforms on the prairies.

Two Arrows then moved to the tipi of his elder sister. His uncle Chief Smoke gave him a spotted pony. Two Arrows began to train to become a warrior. When he was thirteen, Two Arrows went on his first buffalo hunt. He did not seek out the small calves. Two Arrows' first arrow pierced the shoulders of a large bull. When the bull charged, Two Arrows' second shot killed it. The older hunters praised his skill and bravery.

That fall, Chief Smoke led his warriors on a raid. They hoped to steal horses from their traditional enemies, the Crows. Smoke allowed Two Arrows and his best friend, Red Leaf, to join the war party. Their job was to guard the extra horses while Smoke and the others went off to raid the Crows. One night, Two Arrows heard the horses screaming in terror. He raced to the herd on his pony. A grizzly bear stood over a horse it had just killed. With a wild yell, Two Arrows threw his lance as hard as he could.

It sunk deep into the bear's chest. With a swipe of his paw, the bear ripped Two Arrows' leg from ankle to knee. Two Arrows fell to the ground. Quickly he shot two more arrows at the bear. The second arrow hit the grizzly's heart, causing it to fall dead. Two Arrows cleaned his wound. Then he cut off the bear's four-inch claws to make a necklace.

Soon Smoke and the warriors returned with stolen Crow horses. The raiding party then returned home. Two Arrows' grandmother took a gift of beaded moccasins to the medicine man. She suggested that Two Arrows' brave deed had earned him a warrior's name. The medicine man agreed. Two Arrows' new name would be Red Cloud.

Each feather in Red Cloud's war bonnet stood for a brave deed. Often, the bonnet stood on a rack outside his tipi.

RED CLOUD BECOMES AN OGLALA CHIEF

Red Cloud was taller than most Oglalas. He walked with pride and self-assurance. The girls in his camp cast shy glances when he passed. Red Cloud fell in love with a slender girl called Willow Woman (*We-tamahech*). One day, he tied four fine horses outside Willow Woman's tipi. For hours he waited to see if a member of Willow Woman's family sent back the gift. No one did. This meant Willow Woman's father accepted Red Cloud as his daughter's future husband.

Red Cloud and Willow Woman lived in a tipi made of buffalo hide. It was trimmed with painted designs. Outside Willow Woman placed Red Cloud's eagle feather war bonnet on a rack. Each feather stood for a brave deed. Many evenings Red Cloud said his prayers with friends. The smoke from his red clay pipe made Red Cloud feel closer to the Great Spirit.

Red Cloud had many chances to prove he was brave. He also captured many horses on raids against the Crows and Utes. The Oglala measured wealth by the number of horses a person owned. Red Cloud often shared his wealth with those who had less.

A trading post stood on the Laramie River. Each year Red Cloud went there to trade. His wife made a travois, a type of sled, from tipi poles. She tied the front end of the poles to each side of a horse. Then between the poles' rear ends, she piled buffalo skins. Red Cloud traded these skins for red cloth, sugar, and coffee. In 1849 Red Cloud found that the old trading post was now a fort. A new trading post lay a few miles down the North Platte River. Red Cloud's band made the trip down the Medicine Road. They skirted wagons heading west.

Willow Woman and Red Cloud shared a long married life together.

At the trading post, Red Cloud asked what was happening. The trader explained that the whites were heading for Oregon. They called the Medicine Road the Oregon Trail. The Sioux band was not happy. The horses and cattle of the whites ate the grass needed by Sioux ponies. The loud wagon trains scared away the game. And whites brought deadly diseases such as smallpox, measles, and the flu.

Contact with the whites also exposed the Sioux to cholera. This disease originates from contaminated food and drink, and is highly contagious. Many Sioux died within the first twenty-four hours after falling ill. Red Cloud led his band away from the Oregon Trail to the Black Hills. The Oglalas called this sacred ground *Paha Sapa*. Red Cloud went to a mountaintop to pray. He asked the Great Spirit to tell him how to cure the sickness. Red Cloud breathed in the scent of cedar. This was an answer to his prayer. The Sioux stripped the bark and leaves from young cedar trees. They boiled them in clear water to make a strong bitter medicine. The members of Red Cloud's band drank a cup of the medicine every day. Those who were ill became well. No one else fell sick.

Some of the Sioux wanted the fine things they got in trade with the whites. Chief Smoke was one of those who chose to live near the trading posts on the Oregon Trail. Red Cloud disagreed, staying in the wild country far from contact with the whites. Many Sioux followed his lead. Red Cloud was now the real leader of his band.

A NEW TRAIL
CHALLENGES THE SIOUX

In 1862, prospectors first found gold in Montana. The region lay north of the main trails leading west. In 1863, John Bozeman and John Jacobs blazed a new trail to the gold fields. They hoped to make money guiding parties along this new route. It was 400 miles shorter than the old trail and passable for wagons. Since the route was new, there would be enough grass for the travelers' livestock.

Oglala hunters brought word of the new trail to Red Cloud. He was angry about the threat to the Sioux hunting ground. He and some of his warriors rode to see for themselves. Red Cloud studied the marks made by the wagon wheels and iron-shod horses. Just then, John Bozeman and another white settler rode into sight. Red Cloud took them prisoner, but did not kill them. He told Bozeman, "I will let you go back to the Medicine Road (Oregon Trail). But do not come here again."[1] He took their horses, clothes, and supplies. Naked, the two men found their way back to Fort Laramie.

Bozeman and Jacobs went to Deer Creek Crossing on the Oregon Trail. They did not listen to Red Cloud. Instead they signed up wagons to use their trail. Up the trail 150 miles, the first wagons reached Lodgepole Creek. Sioux warriors surrounded the party. They told the whites:

> You can't go in the direction you are going. You are going into our country where we hunt. This is the only good big hunting ground left for us. Your people have taken

In 1863, John Bozeman blazed a new trail to the goldfields of Montana. Soon, wagon trains crossed Sioux lands. They frightened the game and used up the grass.

the rest or scared the game away. We won't let our women and children starve. This is where we make meat. We will keep this land. . . . If you will turn back to the Platte, we will let you go. We will not hurt you. But if you go into our hunting country, our people will wipe you out.[2]

White riders hurried back to Fort Laramie. They returned with a troop of cavalry, which escorted the wagons back to Deer Creek.

The United States government claimed there was peace with the Sioux. They said this because a few friendly bands lived along the Missouri River. In October 1865, their chiefs signed a peace treaty and accepted presents. But no hostile chief "touched the pen." Despite this fact, the government announced it had made peace with all the Sioux bands.

In the meantime, Red Cloud continued to block use of the Bozeman Trail. In the spring of 1866, the Army asked the Oglala chief to come to Fort Laramie. The peace commissioner promised him presents and supplies if he would talk about making peace. Red Cloud led a thousand Oglala to the fort. On June 13, Colonel Henry Carrington arrived at Fort Laramie. He led seven hundred soldiers of the Eighteenth Infantry Regiment. His orders were to build a series of forts on the Bozeman Trail. No one had told the Sioux of these plans.

Red Cloud was angry when he spoke to the peace commissioner. He was dressed in a light blanket and moccasins. His straight black hair reached over his shoulders to his waist. His mouth was a slit beneath a hawk-like nose. His eyes flashed. He accused the whites of pretending to make peace while planning war.

The white men have crowded the Indians back year by year. We are forced to live in a small country north of the Platte. Now, our last hunting ground, the home of the People, is to be taken from us. Our women and children will starve. For my part, I prefer to die fighting rather than by starvation. Great Father sends us presents and wants new road. But White Chief goes with soldiers to steal road before Indian say yes or no![3]

Red Cloud stalked from the room and across the parade ground. Before dawn the next day, the Oglala were gone from Fort Laramie.

RED CLOUD'S WAR

Colonel Carrington's wagon train moved slowly north on the Bozeman Trail. Red Cloud's scouts sized up its strength: Two hundred wagons carried a wealth of supplies. Among the supplies were doors, locks, nails, band instruments, food, and seeds. The party included women, children, servants, and pets.

The Army planned to build two new forts to protect the Bozeman Trail. One would be on the Bighorn River. A second would be on the upper Yellowstone. But these plans didn't work out as hoped. Carrington strengthened Fort Reno on the Powder River. Then he built Fort Phil Kearny at the fork of the Piney River. On the Bighorn in Montana, he built Fort C.F. Smith. But he couldn't build on the upper Yellowstone. His supply of troops wouldn't stretch that far.

Red Cloud knew he and his men couldn't destroy the

forts. Instead the warriors attacked anything moving outside or between the forts. They raided supply trains. And they stole horses and mules whenever possible. Red Cloud's failure to launch a full-scale attack on the forts misled the soldiers. They felt a false sense of security—they didn't think he was serious about waging war.[1] On July 17, 1866, Red Cloud's Oglala stampeded 175 Army horses and mules. The soldiers gave chase over fifteen miles. During the pursuit, the Bluecoats suffered their first casualties. From then on the "Little White Chief," as Red Cloud called Carrington, was under siege.

The Army built Fort Reno on the Powder River in 1865. Colonel Carrington strengthened it in 1866.

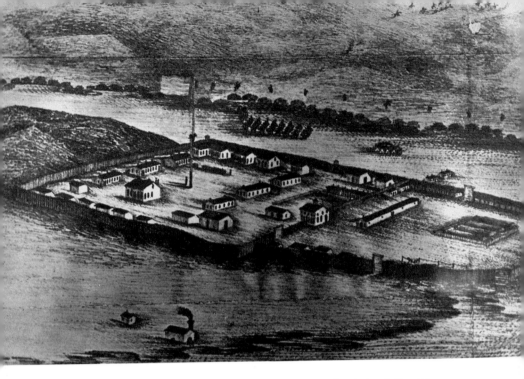

Colonel Carrington built Fort Phil Kearny at the fork of the Piney River. It lay between Forts Reno and C. F. Smith.

Red Cloud gained allies in his fight. Black Bear, an Arapaho chief, brought his warriors for support. Spotted Tail's Brulé Sioux came north to join Red Cloud. Sitting Bull and Gall of the Hunkpapas also joined these tribes. Red Cloud visited the Sioux's old enemies, the Crows. "We want you to aid us in destroying the whites," he said.[2] Young men from the Cheyennes also flocked to Red Cloud's camp. By late summer the Oglala chief led three thousand warriors, though only a few had rifles. They camped along the Tongue River, within striking range of Fort Phil Kearny.

Red Cloud was unlike most war chiefs. He made long-range plans. No war chief had the power to command his men. Red Cloud had to rely on his reputation and oratory to lead his band. Thus he persuaded the warriors to do things his way.

Day after day the siege of Fort Phil Kearny continued. One by one, soldiers were killed while herding livestock, cutting wood, or gathering hay. Fall was turning to winter, and the whites needed wood for fuel. On December 6, Red Cloud's men attacked a party of wood cutters. Carrington led a relief force from the fort. In the following fight the soldiers lost several men.

One of the leaders at the fort hated being on the defensive. Captain William Fetterman claimed "A single company of Regulars could whip a thousand Indians."[3] On December 21, that idea cost him his life.

Red Cloud's victory in the Fetterman Fight brought a quick response. The Army sent a relief force to Fort Phil Kearny. Then blizzards brought deep snow. Neither the soldiers nor the Sioux could move about with ease. No wagon trains tried to use the Bozeman Trail. Red Cloud kept his warriors together. Both sides waited for spring. The government wanted new peace talks. They asked Red Cloud to come to Fort Laramie. He answered promptly; he would not talk of peace until all the soldiers left his hunting grounds.

THE WAR DRAGS ON

Spring came slowly to the besieged forts. There had been no fresh food for months. Most of the soldiers were ill from scurvy. In June the soldiers received new weapons. Seven hundred new breech-loading Springfield rifles replaced the old single-shot muskets. With the fast-loading guns came 100,000 rounds of ammunition. The Army made sure the ammo was not wasted. They fined a soldier 25 cents for any bullet fired without orders. This was a lot of money to a soldier who earned 35 cents a day for building and extra duties.[1]

In July the Sioux and Cheyenne argued over which fort to wipe out first. Red Cloud wanted to attack Fort Phil Kearny. Dull Knife and Two Moon favored Fort C.F. Smith. The Cheyenne had already stripped Fort Smith of its horses. Neither side gave in. So six hundred Cheyenne went north to attack Fort C.F. Smith. On August 1, they attacked a hay-making party. When they charged, the new rifles drove them back, causing heavy losses. A fire they set in the high dry grass failed to burn the fort.

Early the next day Red Cloud attacked at Fort Phil Kearny. His warriors opened fire on a wood-cutting party outside the fort. The soldiers climbed inside their boxlike wagons. Hundreds of Sioux rode closer. They planned to charge while the soldiers reloaded after their first shots. But with the new guns, the soldiers never stopped shooting. Red Cloud's warriors pulled back and regrouped. They charged a second and a third time. Each time their losses were heavy. After a few hours a relief force came from the Fort. Then the Sioux broke ranks and ran. Fire Thunder said later, "It was like green grass withering in a fire. So we picked up our people and went away. I do not know how many of our people were killed, but there were very many. It was bad."[2] The Army called the battle the Wagon Box Fight.

The United States wanted to end the war with Red Cloud. In the years after the Civil War (1861–1865), the country was weary of fighting. Many troops still served in the defeated South. Railroads raced to link their tracks, spanning the nation. By 1867 the Union Pacific tracks reached western Nebraska. There a group of Native Americans spread the tracks apart and waited for a train. When the engine fell on its side, they killed the crew and broke open the "little houses on wheels." The railroad owners demanded that the Army make the land around their railways safe.

A government report urged that a new treaty be made with the Sioux. It stated: "How shall a peace be so easily and so soon made? Simply by retracing our wrong steps and by doing right."[3] A new peace commissioner asked the Sioux to come to Fort Laramie to talk. Only a few

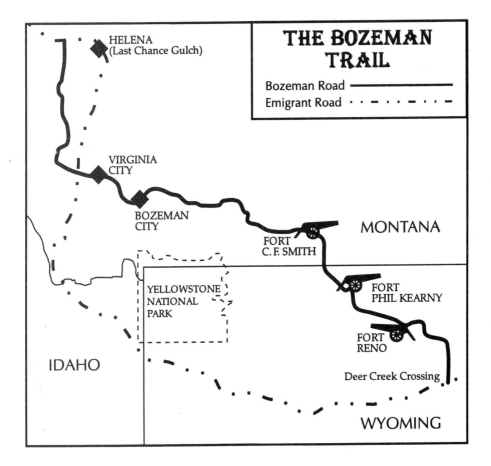

The Bozeman Trail cut through the heart of the Sioux hunting grounds. The U.S. Army built several forts to defend the new road.

bands came. General William T. Sherman told them, "You see [white men] have plenty to eat. They have fine houses and fine clothes. You can have the same. We believe the time has come when you should begin to own these things. We will give you assistance. You can own herds of horses and cattle. . . . You can have cornfields."[4]

Red Cloud did not come to the peace talks. First, he said, the Army must abandon the forts on the Bozeman Trail. Again winter closed in, piling snow against the fort's walls. Sentries kept watch over the white drifts as Red Cloud's war continued.

A SIOUX VICTORY

President Andrew Johnson did not want further fighting. As a result, General William T. Sherman prepared to abandon the forts. He made sure Red Cloud knew of his choice. In August 1868, freighters loaded a wagon train of goods from the forts. Nearby, Red Cloud watched peacefully. When the freight train left Fort C.F. Smith, Red Cloud's warriors entered the fort. Carrying firebrands, they moved from building to building, setting them ablaze. Again at Fort Phil Kearny, they applied torches to everything burnable. Soon the forts that cost the soldiers so many lives were smoking ashes.

The army had abandoned the forts. Still, Red Cloud was in no hurry to sign a peace treaty. He and his warriors spent the next two months hunting. The Sioux needed a large meat supply for the coming winter. On November 4, Red Cloud appeared at Fort Laramie. He brought with him 125 warriors. At the meeting, Red Cloud asked the Army for new guns. His old enemies, the Crows, had the new rifles. But the Army would only give them to tribes that had signed the peace treaty. Red Cloud said that the cause of his war was now removed. He washed his hands with the dust of the floor. Then he made an "X" beside his name.

In August 1868, the Army left the forts on the Bozeman Trail. Fort C.F. Smith was the first to be burned by Red Cloud after it was abandoned.

The defense of Fort Phil Kearny had cost the soldiers many lives. Red Cloud burned it to the ground after the soldiers pulled out.

The other chiefs rose and shook hands with the fort's officers. Red Cloud remained seated. He gave them only the ends of his fingers to shake. It was clear that Red Cloud did not understand the government's Indian policy. He did not know that the treaty called for his people to move onto a reservation. Red Cloud did not allow anyone to explain the peace treaty to him. He said that he "had learned from others all he cared to know about that."[1]

The treaty promised to allow the Sioux to keep most of the Dakota Territory. The area covered all present-day South Dakota west of the Missouri River. The Black Hills were to be kept by the Sioux for as long "as the grass shall grow and the waters shall flow."[2] Within this territory, agencies would serve all the Sioux bands. Whites were banned from this land forever.

In the spring of 1869, Red Cloud arrived at Fort Laramie to trade. With him came a thousand warriors. The agent told him the Sioux must go to Fort Randall to trade. That fort was 300 miles away. Red Cloud refused. He said the bluecoats had agreed to his trading at Fort Laramie when he signed the treaty.

The next year the Commissioner of Indian Affairs asked Red Cloud to come to Washington, D.C. In May Red Cloud and fifteen Oglala began their trip. It took five days riding on their old enemy, the railroad train. Red Cloud found the noise in the cities terrifying. The whites

Red Cloud came to Fort Laramie in November 1868. The treaty he signed promised the Sioux could keep most of the Dakota Territory.

Red Cloud led a delegation of Oglala to the nation's capital in 1870. President Ulysses S. Grant invited Red Cloud to a banquet in the White House.

were as numerous as grasshoppers. Their buildings reached the sky.

President Ulysses S. Grant invited Red Cloud to a banquet at the White House. Rows of quills trimmed Red Cloud's robe. Colorful designs filled his deerskin shirt. More quills and beads ornamented his red leggings. In his hair Red Cloud wore a single eagle feather. President Grant's little daughter Nellie handed him a bouquet. Cabinet members and members of Congress stared at him. Red Cloud stared back. And he stared at the hundreds of blazing candles in the glittering chandeliers. The Sioux liked the White House food. "Surely the white men have many more good things to eat than they send to the Indians," Spotted Tail said.[3]

RED CLOUD GOES TO WASHINGTON

Red Cloud had an ally within the government. Ely Parker was Grant's Commissioner of Indian Affairs. "The Little Father," as he was called, was a Seneca of the Iroquois nation. He had grown up on a New York reservation. Parker took Red Cloud's party on a tour of the capital, the Navy Yard, and the Arsenal. He told them they did not need to wear the tight-fitting black coats and button shoes they had been given. Their buckskins, blankets, and moccasins would be just fine.

On June 9, Red Cloud talked with President Grant in his White House office. Red Cloud wanted to stay near enough to Fort Laramie to trade there. He continued to oppose moving to a reservation on the Missouri River hundreds of miles east or north. He spoke about those who had moved there. "Their children are dying off like sheep. The country does not suit them. . . . They held a paper for me to sign. That is all I got for my land. I know the people you send out there are liars. Look at me. I am poor and naked. I do not want war with my government."[1] President Grant knew the treaty said the Sioux agency was to be at some place on the Missouri. He did not reply directly to Red Cloud. He promised only that the Sioux would be treated justly.

The next day Red Cloud met Secretary of the Interior Jacob Cox. Cox explained the treaty point by point. Red Cloud exclaimed, "This is the first time I have heard of such a treaty. I never heard of it and I do not mean to follow it."[2]

The government sent many Sioux children to school at Carlisle, Pennsylvania, to learn the white man's ways. Many died there from tuberculosis and other diseases.

Red Cloud realized he had been betrayed. That night, in their hotel, some of the Sioux said they were ashamed to go home. They would have to tell their people how they had been deceived.

The next day Secretary Cox gave in. He said that Red Cloud's people did not have to live on a reservation. Instead if they wished, they could live on their hunting grounds. Red Cloud's beloved Powder River lay within the Sioux hunting grounds. For a second time, Red Cloud had won a victory over the government.

Red Cloud next went to New York. At the Cooper Institute he spoke to the people for the first time—not just to officials. The large crowd cheered as he stated his case simply.

> We want to keep the peace. Will you help us? In 1868 men came out and brought papers. We could not read them. They did not tell us truly what was in them. We thought the treaty was to remove the forts. . . . They wanted to send us to traders on the Missouri. We wanted traders where we were. When I reached Washington, the Great Father explained to me what the treaty was. [He] showed me that the interpreters had deceived me. All I want is right and just."[3]

Red Cloud returned to Fort Laramie. He found that local settlers opposed having a Sioux agency anywhere near the Platte Valley. Red Cloud rounded up powerful chiefs from many tribes. They came to a council at Fort Laramie. The Cheyenne sent Dull Knife and Little Wolf.

Others came from the Blackfoot Sioux, the Minneconjous, and the Arapahos. Only Sitting Bull of the Hunkpapas refused to join them. He said, "The white people have put bad medicine over Red Cloud's eyes. [They] make him see everything and anything they please."[4]

At the council the other chiefs agreed with Red Cloud. The agency should be near Fort Laramie. The government gave in and set up a Sioux agency thirty-two miles east of the fort. Red Cloud had won without fighting another war.

Red Cloud toured the country in a Wild West show. In this photograph, Red Cloud (left) appears with Buffalo Bill Cody (center) and American Horse (right).

THE FINAL YEARS

Red Cloud's band camped on the Powder River. They hunted, feasted, and danced. It was almost like the days before the whites came. They resumed their raids to steal horses from other tribes.

The whites did not long honor the Treaty of 1868, which promised the sacred Black Hills to the Sioux forever. In 1874 a gold strike in the Black Hills drew miners by the thousands. Now the government wanted to buy the Black Hills to avoid another war. Red Cloud refused to sell. "The Black Hills are part of the land that is to belong to us 'as long as the grass shall grow.' Does any white man in Washington remember this?"[1]

In September 1875, twenty thousand Sioux met with government agents in a great council. The government offered $6 million for the Black Hills. Red Cloud told them that the Sioux did not want to sell. He named a price he knew the whites would not pay—$600 million. Red Cloud knew that once the Sioux lost their hunting ground, they must become farmers or starve. Red Cloud asked for a house, horses, a cow, pigs, and chickens for each Sioux family. The agents returned to Washington to report their failure. Back in Washington, the agents suggested the government take the Black Hills by force.

Month by month, Red Cloud's status with the tribes declined. They saw him only as a spokesman for peace. He could no longer merge them into a force for war.

In November the government ordered all Sioux onto their reservations by January 31, 1876. Most did not obey. That spring the Army sent three columns of troops to

Red Cloud, shown here with a peace pipe, did not join Sitting Bull and Crazy Horse in their continuing fight for the Black Hills.

drive the Sioux from their homeland. One unit, led by Lieutenant Colonel George Armstrong Custer, met the Sioux on the Little Bighorn River. The Sioux wiped out his troops to the last man.

Red Cloud's heart was with his people. His son Jack joined in the fighting. But Red Cloud took no part in this war. He had seen the whites' cities, and he knew their power and numbers.

By 1877 the Sioux had lost the war. Crazy Horse and his Oglala warriors had surrendered. Sitting Bull's band of Hunkpapas went to Canada. Red Cloud protested when troops came onto the reservation. The soldiers frightened off the game. The soldiers also kept the Sioux from leaving the reservation to hunt. No new supplies came to the agency.

The soldiers made two threats. There would be no food until the Sioux signed away the Black Hills. And the Army might then move the Sioux to the Indian Territory in Oklahoma. Red Cloud's people began to go hungry. To save them from starving, Red Cloud "touched the pen."

Red Cloud was not the chief of all the Sioux. He could not speak for them. His signature had little legal value. Still, it satisfied the whites. The government opened its storehouses. But the food given to the Sioux was of poor quality and in scanty amounts. When Red Cloud tried to hunt in the wild country away from the soldiers, they tracked him down. They marched him back to the agency, holding a gun at his back.

The government built a home for Red Cloud and his family. Located on the Pine Ridge Agency, it had two stories, a fireplace, and glass windows.

In 1878 the government moved the Oglala agency to Pine Ridge. It lay within sight of the Black Hills. Red Cloud tried to keep the Oglala band together. But the government opposed the idea. After a quarrel with the Oglala leader in 1881, the Indian agent no longer recognized Red Cloud as a chief.

Life was hard at Pine Ridge. Red Cloud thought it was a barren waste. Years later Red Cloud said:

> *Most of the [reservation] land is poor and worthless. Think of it! [I] used to own rich soil in a well-watered country so big that I could ride through it in a week on my fastest pony. . . . I have to go five miles for wood for my fire! Washington took our lands and promised to feed and support us. Now I, who used to control five thousand*

warriors, must beg Washington when I am hungry! I must beg for what I own. If I beg hard, they put me in the guard house."[2]

On December 10, 1909, Red Cloud died on the reservation he hated. He was eighty-seven. He will always be remembered as the victor in his war to close the Bozeman Trail.

Red Cloud lived into the 20th century. This picture was taken nine years before his death at age eighty-seven.

NOTES BY CHAPTER

Chapter One

1. Paul and Dorothy Goble, *Brave Eagle's Account of the Fetterman Fight* (New York: Pantheon Books, 1972), p. 41.

2. Ralph K. Andrist, *The Long Death: The Last Days of the Plains Indians* (New York: Macmillan, 1964), p. 108.

3. Andrist, p. 113.

4. Goble, p. 48.

5. Goble, p. 56.

Chapter Two

1. Dorothy Johnson, *Warrior for a Lost Nation* (Philadelphia: Westminster Press, 1969), p. 9.

2. George E. Hyde, *Red Cloud's Folks* (Norman: University of Oklahoma Press, 1937), p. 8.

3. Hyde, p. 29.

Chapter Three

No notes.

Chapter Four

1. Virginia Voight, *Red Cloud: Sioux War Chief* (Champagne, Ill.: Garrard, 1975), p. 42.

2. Dorothy Johnson, *The Bloody Bozeman* (New York: McGraw-Hill, 1971), p. 63.

3. Dee Brown, *Bury My Heart at Wounded Knee* (New York: Holt, Rinehart & Winston, 1970), p. 130.

Chapter Five

1. Alexander Adams, *Sitting Bull* (New York: G.P. Putnam's Sons, 1974), p. 130.

2. Dee Brown, *Bury My Heart at Wounded Knee* (New York: Holt, Rinehart & Winston, 1970), p. 133.

3. Adams, p. 133.

Chapter Six

1. Dorothy Johnson, *The Bloody Bozeman* (New York: McGraw-Hill, 1971), p. 273.

2. John Neihardt, *Black Elk Speaks* (Lincoln: University of Nebraska Press, 1961), p. 17.

3. Alexander Adams, *Sitting Bull* (New York: G.P. Putnam's Sons, 1974), p. 155.

4. Adams, p. 159.

Chapter Seven

1. Alexander Adams, *Sitting Bull* (New York: G.P. Putnam's Sons, 1974), p. 176.

2. Sheila Black, *Sitting Bull and the Battle of Little Big Horn* (Englewood Cliffs, N.J.: Silver Burdett, 1989), p. 71.

3. Dee Brown, *Bury My Heart at Wounded Knee* (New York: Holt, Rinehart & Winston, 1970), p. 184.

Chapter Eight

1. Dee Brown, *Bury My Heart at Wounded Knee* (New York: Holt, Rinehart & Winston, 1970), pp. 184–185.

2. Brown, p. 186.

3. Brown, p. 187.

4. Brown, p. 188.

Chapter Nine

1. Virginia Voight, *Red Cloud: Sioux War Chief* (Champagne, Ill.: Garrard, 1975), pp. 70–71.

2. Dorothy Johnson, *The Bloody Bozeman* (New York: McGraw-Hill, 1971), p. 311.

GLOSSARY

agency—The site of government offices on a reservation.

band—A subdivision of a tribe, sometimes only a few dozen in number.

chief—A leader of a band or tribe; often a chief was limited to a specific role, such as leadership in war.

council—A meeting of the adults in a tribe; all warriors had the right to express their opinions.

medicine man—A Native American priest. Medicine men often combined foretelling the future with practicing medicine.

reservation—An area set aside by the government to be the permanent home of a group of Native Americans.

scouts—Skilled Native Americans or frontiersmen who served as lookouts, read tracks, found trails, and located game for the U.S. Army or pioneer groups.

scurvy—A disease caused by a diet lacking in ascorbic acid (vitamin C).

tipi—The home of the Sioux; lodges were made of hide stretched over many poles.

touch the pen—A Native American term for signing a treaty.

treaties—Agreements between two governments; treaties between Native Americans and whites often dealt with the sale of land.

tribe—A large group of Native Americans, speaking a common language and living in the same area.

warrior—An adult Native American fighting man.

MORE GOOD READING ABOUT
══════RED CLOUD══════

Adams, Alexander. *Sitting Bull.* New York: G.P. Putnam's Sons, 1974.

Andrist, Ralph K. *The Long Death, The Last Days of The Plains Indians.* New York: Macmillan, 1964.

Black, Sheila. *Sitting Bull and the Battle of Little Big Horn.* Englewood Cliffs, N.J.: Silver Burdett, 1989.

Brown, Dee. *Bury My Heart at Wounded Knee.* New York: Holt, Rinehart & Winston, 1970.

Goble, Paul and Dorothy Goble. *Brave Eagle's Account of the Fetterman Fight.* New York: Pantheon Books, 1972.

Hyde, George E. *Red Cloud's Folks.* Norman, Okla.: University of Oklahoma, Press, 1937.

Johnson, Dorothy. *The Bloody Bozeman.* New York: McGraw-Hill, 1971.

Johnson, Dorothy. *Warrior for a Lost Nation.* Philadelphia: Westminster Press, 1969.

Neihardt, John. *Black Elk Speaks.* Lincoln, Neb.: University of Nebraska Press, 1961.

Voight, Virginia. *Red Cloud: Sioux War Chief.* Champaign, Ill.: Garrard, 1975.

INDEX

A
Arapaho, 23

B
Black Bear, 23
Black Hills (Paha Sapa), 16,
 31, 38–39, 40
Bozeman Trail, 4, 17, 19, 21,
 24, 28, 42

C
Carrington, Col. Henry, 7,
 19, 21, 24
Cheyennes, 23, 25, 36
Cox, Sec. Jacob, 35, 36
Crazy Horse, 7, 40
Custer, Lt. Col. George, 40

D
Dull Knife, 36

F
Fetterman, Capt. William,
 7–8, 24
Fetterman Fight, 4, 7–9, 24
Fort C. F. Smith, 21, 25–26,
 29
Fort Laramie, 19, 20, 24, 27,
 29, 31, 32, 34, 36, 37
Fort Phil Kearny, 5, 21, 23,
 24, 25, 26, 29

Fort Reno, 21

G
Grant, Ulysses S., 33, 34, 35

J
Johnson, Andrew, 29

L
Lewis and Clark, 11
Little Wolf, 36
Lodgepole Creek, 18
Lone Man, 10

O
Oglala Sioux
 life on the reservation,
  39–42
 origins, 10–11
 way of life, 11, 14, 15
Oregon Trail (Medicine
 Road), 16, 18

P
Parker, Comm. Ely, 34
Pine Ridge, 41
Powder River, 38

R
Red Cloud
 appearance, 14, 20

attacks Fort Phil
    Kearny, 7–9, 26
attacks supply trains,
    22
bear fight, 12–13
birth, 10
and the Black Hills,
    38–39, 40
blocks Bozeman Trail,
    19
burns Fort C. F. Smith,
    29
burns Fort Phil Kearny,
    29
childhood, 11–13
death, 42
at the Fetterman Fight,
    7–9
at Fort Laramie, 19,
    20, 24, 29, 31, 32,
    36
joins raid on Crows, 12
learns contents of
    treaty, 35–36
as medicine man, 16
parents' death, 11
prevented from hunting,
    40
removed as chief, 41
sees Oregon Trail, 16

signs treaty of 1868,
    30–31
visits New York City, 36
visits Washington, D.C.,
    32–33, 34–36
warns Bozeman, 17
wins agency at Fort
    Laramie, 37
Red Cloud, Jack, 40

S
Sherman, Gen. William T.,
    27–28, 29
Sitting Bull, 37, 40
Smoke, Chief, 10, 12, 13, 16

T
Ten Eyck, Capt. Tenedor, 9
Treaty of 1865, 19
Treaty of 1868, 38
Two Arrows. *See* Red Cloud.

U
Union Pacific, 26

W
Wagon Box Fight, 26
Walks-As-She-Thinks, 10
Willow Woman, 14